THE BATSFORD COLOUR BOOK OF
Stately Homes

Introduction and commentaries by
E. R. Chamberlin

B. T. BATSFORD LTD LONDON

First published 1973

© E. R. Chamberlin 1973

Made and printed in Great Britain by William Clowes, Beccles, Suffolk,
for the publishers B. T. Batsford Ltd, 4 Fitzhardinge Street, London W1

ISBN 0 7134 0025 0

Contents

Acknowledgments

The Publishers wish to thank the following for permission to reproduce
the photographs appearing in this book:
Aero Films Ltd for page 17
Noel Habgood for pages 19, 29 and 63
A. F. Kersting for pages 21, 23, 25, 27, 31, 33, 37, 39, 41, 43, 45, 47, 49,
    51, 53, 55, 57, 59 and 61
Kenneth Scowen for page 35

Introduction

'Stately home' – the phrase has not yet been blessed by the Oxford English Dictionary but it is a very useful term, identifying adequately enough a richly varied class of residence which can be anything from a modest manor house to a fullscale castle. But there is an ambivalence about the phrase, a kind of wry self-mockery that is very much a product of this century. On the one hand there is undoubtedly something incongruous about the idea of a building which, created precisely to demonstrate and preserve power and privilege, competes now with its peers for the pennies of the masses. On the other hand, an age which has elevated the concept of total equality to the status of a moral law is reluctant to recognise that privilege might have indeed produced excellence, that Jack might not perhaps be as good as his master. So the half-mocking, half-envious phrase passes into general currency, faithfully reflecting a period of social fragmentation and unease.

But the stately home has always reflected social change, unlike its great companion, the church, which rapidly found a final form and so journeyed down the centuries essentially unchanged. The changes can be detected in the name which the building uses to describe itself. 'Palace' is rare – very rare indeed apart from royal buildings. 'Castle' is a survival from the older, primitive period: Arundel, Berkeley, Warwick – all are genuinely military structures which have – as it were absent-mindedly – become homes. 'Manor' describes a once vital function – the great house as a generator and reservoir of rural wealth: it was only later, in the eighteenth century, that its role as consumer of wealth dominated the other two. 'Hall' is simply the description of a form or structure – the barn-like building which once served as a kind of tribal meeting place, became a nucleus and finally a fossil. 'Abbey' or 'Priory' indicates the great plunder of the sixteenth century. 'House' marks that prudent English tendency to play down possessions so that the rich man will use the same term for his vast mansion as the poor man uses for his lean-to hovel.

But what ever the type or the age or the size of the structure, a characteristic of each is that it is a home. A few of the houses, like Ham House in Surrey, are, strictly, museums – places owned and administered by an official body, locked up each nightfall to stand empty and lonely through the hours of darkness. But in most of them, the untidy, casual, comfortable business of family life is being carried on somewhere beyond the red ropes and the table laid for state banquets. Some of the families have established themselves only comparatively recently as tenants, perhaps, of the official body which owns the house. But, astonishingly, some of the families are coeval with the houses they inhabit: the Berkeleys have been living in Berkeley Castle for over eight centuries, the Russells at Woburn since they first acquired it in the sixteenth century.

The concept of the great house is rooted deep in human society for it is simply the concept of the family, grouped together for protection and mutual comfort in an indifferent or actively hostile world. In Europe, it took specific shape during the long night that followed the break-up of the Carolingian empire, the last attempt at European unity. Society fragmented again into its basic units – the family and its associates. A strong, determined man constructs a building a little larger, a little easier to defend than the huts of his neighbours and, as a good neighbour should, he shares that protection with those who cannot build their own. They, in return for that shield in the perilous days, gratefully till his fields or fight for him and from that hesitant, pragmatic beginning, the complex pyramidal structure of feudalism came into being.

England had established its basic unit, the manor, long before the Norman Conquest, so that William had an easy means to hand to reward his followers. Each manor could have only one lord, but a lord could have many manors, depending on his strength, his standing with the king, and his unscrupulousness. Until the great age of exploration and the subsequent expansion of trade, it was from the manor and its ecclesiastical companion, the monastery, that all wealth was drawn, for they alone were equipped to process the raw material of the planet. The monastery was destined to disappear, but so deep was the imprint which the manor placed upon society that the impression lasts today despite the arterial road that gouges through it and the housing estate that masks its outline.

The manor formed an economic unit composed of church, labourers' cottages, agricultural fields and the manor house itself. Apart from the church, the hall of the manor was the only building to be constructed of permanent materials. The surviving halls of this earlier period – for example, that of Oakham Castle, built about 1180 – are virtually indistinguishable from the nave of a church. The Normans knew only one way to span their enormous stone structures and the low, rounded arch on its stocky pillar was as common in domestic as in ecclesiastic building. It was not until the thirteenth century that there occurred the architectural breakthrough of the open timber roof, enabling the builder to carry the hall up to dizzy heights.

In the two centuries following the Conquest the great house was, essentially, a defended farm-house: all other functions were ancillary to the business of raising and storing agricultural produce and protecting it, and the painfully cultivated farm-lands, from the depredations of the powerful and the greedy. The owners did not automatically fortify their houses: permission had to be obtained from the monarch, who granted his license only reluctantly, for each fortified building created a potential centre of opposition. But it was hard to resist the pleas to create legitimate defence: as late as the 1470s the Edgecumbes were driven out of Cothele House in Cornwall by powerful and hostile neighbours. The moats and towers and gatehouses and machicolations, which were to give these buildings their powerful romantic appeal, continued to be built until well into the sixteenth century.

Nevertheless, as early as the mid-thirteenth century – specifically, during the reign of Henry III – another function was added to the traditional functions of defence and production: the more wealthy, more aesthetic owners began to treat their uncompromising structures as homes and indulged in a little cautious decorating. The major advance, for the very wealthy, was the use of glass in windows: hitherto, the residents put up with the draughts or kept the wind out with sheets or horn and waxed linen. Now a few magnates, like Sir Walter Poultney at Penshurst in 1340, inserted expensive glass in the walls. Most of these windows were detachable so that their owner could carry them, like tapestries, from manor to manor, and the glass in some of them could have been little less opaque than horn. But it was a beginning. Poultney still sturdily clung to the tradition of the open hearth in the centre of the hall whence the smoke found its way out – sometimes – through a hole in the roof. But other men followed the king's lead and introduced the new-fangled fireplace.

The Great Hall was still the centre of all social life whenever darkness or bad weather kept the household indoors. Even in houses which boasted of tapestried walls, windows of glass and reasonable efficient fireplaces with real chimneys, the floor was commonly of beaten earth with rushes strewn upon it. This area became to be known, significantly, as the marsh, and even in the early sixteenth century the fastidious Erasmus was describing, with disgust, exactly what lay under the current layer of fresh rushes. At one end of the hall a screen cut off the entrance door and the service quarters. The innately conservative English were to retain this screen long after the domestic arrangements had become sophisticated: it provided the ideal base for the elaborate Elizabethan and Jacobean decorations. At the other end of the hall was the raised dais for the master, the immediate family and honoured guests while a door gave access to the bower – the attractively named drawing room for the ladies – and the solar – the room on the first floor which was also used as a bedroom. Rooms were made simply by dividing up the interior space, with no provision made for passages: privacy was a very rare luxury indeed, with each room acting as a passage to the next.

During the second half of the fifteenth century there began the first, tentative movements towards a planned, architectural construction. Until that period, the tendency was to build *ad hoc*, adding on out-buildings as they became necessary, adapting, expanding. The use of brick became increasingly popular: cheaper and easier to use than stone, it conferred permanence on structures which hitherto would be expected to collapse within a generation. But at the same time the combination of lath and plaster and half-timber was also developed: this was to achieve its flowering in the late sixteenth century with the bold black-and-white half-timbered houses such as the fantastic Moreton Old Hall in Cheshire. The half-timbered house was, in effect, a complex skeleton or scaffold whose interstices were filled with the lath and plaster – flimsy materials through which a strong man could drive a hole easily enough and yet astonishingly capable of surviving, century after century, distorted a little in shape but sound in substance.

In 1485 occurred the Battle of Bosworth, a battle which not only brought the Wars of the Roses to an end but marked a moment of change in English history as precise if not as dramatic as the Conquest itself. The heroic period now lay in the past: the future would lay with statesmen and merchants and financiers rather than with soldiers. The new king, Henry VII, summed up the qualities of the new age in his own person, preferring to fine rather than to imprison, eager to invest in anything that would show a profit: avaricious, parsimonious – but also imaginative enough to finance a Cabot. The coming men resembled their monarch: no longer was it deemed beneath a gentleman's dignity to trade when trade could bring in such immense and glittering rewards. Suddenly, a swarm of new families were pushing aside the old aristocracy – Cavendish, Cecil, Russell, Thynne, making their fortunes through a skilful combination of commerce and political astuteness.

Traditionally, the most obvious and easiest way to demonstrate the possession of great wealth and power has always been to build a palace or mansion: the more settled the period, the more splendid the building, for the owner can not only indulge his fancy, secure in the protection of the law, but wealth that would otherwise be diverted to defence can be lavished on ornament. The Tudor period faithfully followed tradition. Those men who could afford to do so abandoned their castles and built anew, following the example set by the wealthy newcomers, such as the Cecils, whose founder, Lord Burghley, built the great mansion of Burghley House.

The most evident characteristic of the new kind of house is the generous area devoted to windows, clearest indication of the increased private wealth which could afford to buy hundreds of square yards of expensive glass, and the increased social stability which permitted domestic life to be carried on behind so frail a barrier. Battlements and gate-towers still continued to be built, but more as a continuance of tradition than from any real belief in their military necessity. Inside, perhaps the biggest change was the shift from the ground floor to the first floor. The Great Hall still continued to be built and used, but more and more the state apartments were to be found situated in the Italian manner. This, in turn, had an effect upon the placing and elaborating of the staircase. Hitherto, it was simply a means to pass from the lower to the upper floors: now, giving access as it did to the ceremonial rooms, it became a major architectural feature in its own right, as in that majestic flight of stairs at Hardwick Hall. The perfecting of fireplaces produced two more features for decoration: outside, the chimney was carved, sculpted, twisted into the most fantastic shapes, giving the Tudor roof-line its characteristic romantic appearance of some gothic forest in stone. Inside, the fireplace became a towering piece of sculpture in which the hearth itself seems almost an afterthought. At a house near Bath Elizabeth's godson, Sir John Harington, proudly displayed an innovation – an efficient water-closet. He even rushed into print, singing its praises and describing its operation, together with a charming little illustration of

A godly Father sitting on a draught,
Doing what God and nature hath him taught.

But the general public preferred to continue to make do with the traditional noisome privies.

Some time in the 1560s an Italian craftsman, John of Padua by name, took a hand in the building of Sir William Thynne's house at Longleat in Wiltshire and so marked a moment of change in English architecture – the architect had arrived. It is impossible to say exactly what the Italian contributed to Longleat, and neither did he leave any school or followers to carry on distinctively whatever he might have originated.

Doubtless, other aristocratic builders had used architects to guide them in their enthusiasm but, by a quirk of history, John of Padua's name was the first to be recorded as that of a professional working to the instructions of a layman. Nearly a generation was to pass before another professional, Inigo Jones, dominated in the annals of the craft. Jones was born in 1573 – in the same year as Ben Johnson – the son of a Smithfield clothworker. He was in Italy as early as 1597, returning there three more times in the next decade, drawing upon the well-spring of the Renaissance. James I appointed him surveyor-general of the royal buildings in 1612 and it was in that capacity that, in 1615, he designed the first-known of his buildings in England – the Banqueting Hall in Whitehall. His influence was wide, but even so, the architect remained something of a rarity, building remaining largely in the hands of master masons. Jones's contemporary, Sir Roger Pratt, bitterly noted that 'Architecture here has not received the advantages which it has in other parts, it continuing almost still as rude here as it was at the very first.'

Architecture faithfully reflected the great social changes of the mid-seventeenth century. The great Elizabethan and Jacobean mansions – Hardwick, Burleigh, Knole and the rest – though scarcely a generation old, were already old-fashioned. They had been built by immensely wealthy people to entertain – and impress – the monarch. Now, rising prices, less capital and the emergence of a new middle class led imperceptibly to the building of less ostentatious houses. There were exceptions such as the enormous pile of Wilton House, built by the Earl of Pembroke at the suggestion of Charles I – who made it possible by showering his favourite with sinecures: but in general the typical Caroline house was built for the gentry rather than the aristocracy. In compensation for the loss of size was an increased opulence in interior decorating. New skills and techniques took final form after the Restoration so that the last three decades of the seventeenth century was the Golden Age of English craftsmanship, particularly in woodcarving and plasterwork. The urbane John Evelyn discovered young Grinling Gibbons and set him on the path to fame and a modest fortune, in his wake the great houses of England blossoming in those incredibly delicate, detailed carvings of fruit and flowers. Walls and ceilings broke into a riot of plasterwork. Hitherto, the great ceilings had been cast in sections and nailed up while semi-plastic: now the development of a new, quick-drying plaster – stucco duro – allowed the most elaborate work, even involving undercutting. Painting played a secondary role as though the builders were reluctant to draw too much attention to themselves, preferring to express themselves in sumptuous but noncommital carving and plasterwork.

Confidence and arrogance came back with a flourish in the eighteenth century. The Enclosure Acts vastly increased the income of the country gentry at a time when it was fashionable to have aesthetic interests. Throughout, the English aristocracy had prudently avoided the path that their French counterpart had taken. A figure like the Duke of Somerset with his almost pathological snobbery, his almost frantic attempts to avoid contact with the lower classes was an anomaly, a rarity. The Restoration dramatists certainly treated the provincial landowner as a stock figure of fun but outside the tiny, artificial world of the metropolis the English ruling classes boasted of their rural origins and spent the greater part of their lives in places and pursuit which brought the classes into intimate and daily contact with each other.

In the eighteenth century, however, the injection of wealth produced a kind of architectural megalomania where the greater the acreage tamed and covered, the more esteemed the architect. It is now that the park comes into its own – the product of the landscape gardener, gifted with the ability to see years or decades into the future and so convince his employer that an avenue of yew or a grove of oaks should be here rather than there. The landscape gardener briefly shares the glamour of the architect and is identifiable by name and style. Wise, who forced nature into the formal patterns sanctioned by Le Nôtre; Humphrey Repton who immortalised his work in exquisite little sketches: William Kent, of whom Walpole said 'He leaped the fence and saw that all nature was a garden'; and the doyen of them all, Lancelot Brown, who gained the slightly comical nickname of Capability and whose name must occur with monotonous regularity in any study of the period.

Coincident with the rise of landscape gardening, 'stately home' visiting begins on a large scale. The aristocracy expected, as a matter of course, to receive the hospitality of their peers while travelling, but now anybody with the right connections could get permission to enter almost any great house. The owner of some great mansion built by a nationally or internationally famous architect and packed with rare sculptures and books and paintings, tended to look upon himself as a kind of custodian rather than an exclusive owner. And some of the visitors who made the rounds kept records which were to prove historically priceless, like those of the indefatigible Celia Fiennes who had something sprightly and apposite to say about every place she visited.

The rising tide of egalitarianism began to submerge the great house during the First World War, and in the years following the Second World War heavy taxation – in particular ferocious death duties – almost completed the task. Yet, with that compromise which the British have raised to an art form, destruction has been partial, not total. The life-style continues, if on a greatly restricted level, nourished perhaps by candyfloss stalls and elephant rides and government grants but still viable and distinctive, the stately home remaining a home and not a museum.

BLENHEIM PALACE, OXFORDSHIRE

The British have never been over-eager to honour military heroes – a statue or a plaque with, perhaps, a pension is usually considered more than adequate. Blenheim Palace is a resounding exception to this thrifty rule, token of the nation's sense of relief and pride after the Blenheim victory of 1704. Queen Anne provided the land, Parliament raised the money and in 1705 John Vanbrugh began the task of raising an immense palace for the first Duke of Marlborough.

Vanbrugh lost the second battle of Blenheim – that with the duke's redoubtable wife, Sarah. He resigned in a rage in 1716, and when Marlborough died Sarah was left a vast sum and power 'to spoil Blenheim in her own way', as Vanbrugh put it bitterly. She was involved with lawsuits with 401 people connected with the building of Blenheim and by the end of her life had spent £300,000 on the palace, three times Vanbrugh's estimate. But she finished the enormous building.

COMPTON WYNYATES, WARWICKSHIRE

Brick, the most prosaic and proverbially the most solid of materials, has been metamorphosised here into the medium for a floating fantasy. The Comptons were lords of the manor from the early thirteenth century but did not begin the present building until the mid-fifteenth century. Even then, work lagged for another half-century – a fortunate procrastination, for the unknown architect who gave the house its final form in the early sixteenth century drew upon the experience of more than a generation of English builders for whom brick was the only true building material. Building tradition dies hard and Compton Wynyates was provided with a keep, complete with battlements, long after such fortifications had become museum pieces. The family were on the wrong side in the Civil War and Parliamentary troops caused heavy damage to the building in 1644: the house remained partly destroyed until the nineteenth century, when it was restored and embellished with the extraordinary topiary garden.

KEDLESTON HALL, DERBYSHIRE

Kedleston is very much an architect's building, the ground plan rigorously following a somewhat dauntingly symmetrical ideal: a centre block is surrounded by four satellite pavilions, connected to the main block by passageways. Such, at least, is the theory and how far the eighteenth century architect was prepared to go in the name of symmetry is demonstrated by the fact that one of the separated pavilions contains the kitchen, infallibly ensuring that all food will be stone-cold by the time it appears in the gorgeous state dining room.

The symmetry of Kedlestone is all the more remarkable considering that its building took place under the supervision of three successive architects – Brettingham, who began it in 1758, Paine and finally Robert Adam. Inevitably it was Adam who left his powerful classical imprint upon the building – in particular the remarkable Hall. As part of a home it perhaps lacks something: as a reproduction of an ideal Roman building it has everything.

CHATSWORTH, DERBYSHIRE

This most English of country houses was designed by a Dutchman, William Talman, in 1687 for the first Duke of Devonshire. Talman used a beautiful local stone which, over the years, has mellowed and weathered to blend into a landscape that is itself a subtle blend of the natural and the cultivated. Purists argue that Talman's siting of the state rooms on the first floor gives an overbalanced effect but they do humanise what might otherwise be an over correct classical facade. These state apartments form one of the most splendid of Stuart suites in existence with a riot of carved decorations by Samuel Watson. The gardens display what is virtually a Latin love of fountains which fascinated contemporaries: 'There is one basin in the middle of one garden thats very large and by sluces beside the Images several pipes plays out yet water – some fflush it up that it ffroth like Snow.' Another elaborate water organ created a kind of living arch or tunnel of water, while what seemed from a distance to be an ordinary willow tree, proved on close up to be a fantastically complex fountain with apertures for water in every leaf.

LITTLE MORETON HALL, CHESHIRE

This is undoubtedly the most famous of the dramatic black-and-white houses of the Midlands, and the most distinctive part of this highly distinctive building is the gatehouse overlooking the moat. Originally, it consisted of two stories only, but when the Moretons wanted to add a fashionable Long Gallery to their home they decided to place it on top of the gatehouse. It runs the entire length of the range, made up of windows for the most part and giving the gatehouse the appearance of towering height. Behind the gatehouse the mansion proper forms two sides of a square, the third side being left open.

Building of the Hall probably began about 1520 and was carried on by three generations of Moretons in a comfortably casual manner, the last major addition being in 1580 when the Long Gallery was built. The impression conveyed to a visitor standing in the courtyard is of an almost overwhelming richness of lead and glass and carved wood but, nevertheless, the human scale is never lost. The place was a home, built by local craftsmen – like that Richard Dale, carpenter, who put up a range of windows in 1559 and proudly carved his name to commemorate the fact.

CASTLE HOWARD, YORKSHIRE

The commission to design Castle Howard was the means whereby Sir John Vanbrugh was able to abandon playwriting for the more lucrative business of architecture. The immensely wealthy third Earl of Carlises had already engaged Talman as architect – but Vanbrugh was a fellow clubman of the Earl's and poor Talman was quietly edged to one side.

Work was begun in 1702 after two years of protracted discussion, and was still unfinished when Vanbrugh died 24 years later. Vanbrugh not only specialised in the colossal, but also had a neat turn of hand with dainty little buildings and he dotted his lodges and garden gates about Castle Howard. But it was Hawksmoor who built the great Mausoleum which, Horace Walpole claimed, 'would tempt one to be buried alive'. The Castle is still a home – but is also one of the great museums of the country. The Costume Galleries, set up in the eighteenth-century stable block, contain the largest private collection of dress from the seventeenth to the twentieth centuries.

ALNWICK CASTLE, NORTHUMBERLAND

In addition to Alnwick, the Dukes of Northumberland owned Albury House in Surrey and Syon House in Middlesex, but this 'large beutifull and portlie castell' on the banks of the river Alne is the seat of the Percys and has been since 1309. The castle began life as border stronghold in the twelfth century, a reasonably secure place for a Norman outpost among very hostile neighbours. The earlier form would have been a simple motte-and-bailey construction but in the fourteenth century it was considerably enlarged when the existing walls were built. It remained a home after it had ceased to be a military emplacement, and in the eighteenth century Robert Adam was given a free hand with the interior decoration, producing his usual richly elegant effect which must have contrasted strangely with the craggy exterior. In the mid-nineteenth century, however, the current Duke unleashed Anthony Salvin on the castle and he, with the decorator's impatience for his predecessor's work, swept much of Adam's interior away.

HOLKHAM HALL, NORFOLK

Work on Holkham Hall did not start until 1734, although Thomas Coke of Holkham had been turning over in his mind the idea of building a Roman-style house for at least 16 years – ever since he had met Lord Burlington and William Kent while travelling in Italy.

Kent became Coke's architect and set about the business of transferring Rome to Norfolk. Essentially, Kent's task was less that of an originator than that of a highly sensitive synthesiser, combining elements not only from the original Roman models but also from such Renaissance adaptors as Palladio and Inigo Jones.

He was astonishingly successful, creating something which demonstrated its classical origins in every line but which was also individual and of its own period. The exterior is dignified – austere – but the interior superb. Unforgettable is the glowing marble entrance hall, built like a Roman basilica, with a soaring flight of steps leading to the saloon on the main floor.

OXBURGH HALL, NORFOLK

Here is a building that has successfully combined the dual, and frequently conflicting roles, of military defence and domestic comfort. At a casual glance, Oxburgh seems to resemble more closely a collegiate building rather than a castle, but on a closer inspection it becomes evident that the towering gatehouse, the machicolations and the deep moat are not there for aesthetic purposes. Oxburgh was built in 1482, just three years before the Battle of Bosworth brought the Wars of the Roses to an end. Its owner, Sir Edmund Bedingfield, was a personal friend of Richard III but suffered no disadvantage as a result of Richard's defeat at Bosworth. Henry VII, indeed, seems to have been sufficiently certain of Bedingfield's somewhat elastic loyalty to become his guest at Oxburgh.

The Hall remained in the hands of the Bedingfields until 1952, a continuous occupation of nearly five centuries. It is now the property of the National Trust, to whom it was given by the Dowager Lady Bedingfield.

BURTON AGNES HALL, YORKSHIRE

Among devotees of the occult, Burton Agnes is best known for the singular story of the skull of 'Owd Nance' – Frances Griffiths, daughter of the first owner who died while the Hall was in process of construction. So eager was she to see the finished building that she left instructions that her skull was to be kept in the house – and would create a noisy disturbance if ever removed.

So the legend: Frances' father, Sir Henry Griffith, built Burton Agnes between 1598 and 1610. He seems to have been a sturdy conservative, ignoring the exuberance of the new-fangled Renaissance style, adapting the soberer style of his forebears to create an elegant, admirably proportioned home that somehow looks like a very large and superior dolls' house. 'It looks finely in the approach,' noted that indefatigible traveller Celia Fiennes. She was much impressed with the great gate-houses and the bowling green 'palisaded round'. Posterity finds more to admire in the interior, particularly the elaborate hall screen with its wealth of allegorical figures in low relief.

HEVENINGHAM HALL, SUFFOLK

This imposing mansion neatly illustrates the manner in which a fashion-conscious landowner, finding himself the happy possessor of an expanding income, informed the world of his good fortune and joined the ranks of the cultured élite. The previous Heveningham Hall was a plain, workaday home from which a prosperous estate had been very adequately run but which would not have attracted a second glance from Celia Fiennes. In 1778 the owner, Sir Gerard Vanneck, engaged Sir Robert Taylor to refurbish the Hall on modern lines. Taylor retained the existing building but clad it in a kind of stone shell and added two wings both to give balance and increase guest accommodation. Taylor died when the constructional work was completed but before the decoration was begun – a fortunate timing from the view of the owner, because the man who finished the work was James Wyatt, the only truly successful follower of the highly idiosyncratic Adam brothers. In his hands the noble classical proportions of the Adam style was retained but in some subtle manner turned into an essentially English style. Wyatt's interiors are not reproduced Roman houses but English houses decorated in the Roman manner. And in the gardens, the ubiquitous Capability Brown created a landscape that was the living counterpart of Wyatt's interior work.

KIRBY HALL, NORTHAMPTONSHIRE

This beautiful building is now in the care of the Department of the Environment, for it is almost wholly a ruin. Its careful preservation reflects the current preoccupation regarding the care of ancient monuments – renovation rather than restoration: although visually a ruin the surviving stonework is in superb condition.

Thomas Thorpe probably built the house for Sir John Stafford between 1570 and 1575 – although Thorpe's habit of making meticulous drawings of any architecture that took his fancy makes it difficult to ascribe Kirby to him without an element of doubt. Thorpe's employer did not have long to enjoy the house for, shortly after its completion, he sold it to Sir Christopher Hatton, the friend of Lord Burghley who, in friendly rivalry, was building his own great mansion near Stamford. The house remained in the hands of the Hattons and their descendants, the Finches, until the early nineteenth century. But a gradually accumulating burden of debts forced the tenth Earl of Winchelsea simply to abandon the house. It is a testimony to the skill of the builders that, though uninhabited for over a century, Kirby was still worthwhile renovating in 1929 when it came into the hands of the Ministry of Works.

HATFIELD HOUSE, HERTFORDSHIRE

Most of the great houses tend to draw away from established communities, creating their own centre of gravity. Hatfield, however, is almost an integral part of the nearby village.

This is one of the first houses to be specifically associated with an architect – Robert Lyminge, who began its construction in 1607 for the Earl of Salisbury. The Hatfield Papers, however, make clear that the architect was still not the final arbiter but had to share his authority with a large number of master-craftsmen, each of whom had very firm opinions about what was desirable in his own sphere. They seemed to have worked well together, however, for they kept well within Lyminge's estimate of £8,500 for the whole construction. The Earl's father was that William Cecil, Lord Burghley, who served Elizabeth so well over 40 years – and amassed a big enough fortune to build his own huge mansions of Burghley and Theobalds. Elizabeth spent her childhood in the older hall at Hatfield.

WOBURN ABBEY, BEDFORDSHIRE

There is nothing in the least ecclesiastical about Woburn Abbey. It simply stands on the site of a Cistercian monastery whose abbot was incautious enough to make an uncomplimentary remark about Anne Boleyn. After his execution the Abbey was given to John, first earl of Bedford.

The old monastic buildings were torn down in the 1620s and a handsome house raised on the site. Most of this was demolished in the eighteenth century and the present building is one of Henry Flitcroft's grandiose structures, built about 1745.

Woburn today is famous – or notorious – for its wholehearted dedication to the Stately Home Trade, with almost every conceivable kind of outdoor entertainment laid on. But behind the fairground atmosphere is a richly beautiful house that sums up the wealth of eighteenth-century England. Flitcroft excelled himself in this ornate State Dining-room where even priceless works of art seem to be just another kind of wall covering.

ASHDOWN HOUSE, BERKSHIRE

The eye would probably pass over Ashdown House if it were built in, say, Mayfair or Bloomsbury, for there it would have been entirely reasonable to build a tall thin house and so make fullest use of limited ground space. But why should the first Lord Craven build a five-storey house, complete with basement, in the depths of the country as though he were hemmed in by neighbours? History gives no answer, and even legend is silent. Ashdown House stands as evidence of that amiable eccentricity which is a characteristic of the English aristocracy.

Craven was one of the fortunate men whose loyalty to Charles I cost him only a period of exile. During exile he struck up that acquaintance with the aunt of Charles II, Elizabeth of Bohemia, which led to so much speculation among their contemporaries. Abandoned by almost everybody else in England she found a rare and constant friend in Craven.

Ashdown's architect was John Webb who, together with Inigo Jones, designed the splendours of Wilton House.

SYON HOUSE, MIDDLESEX

This is another of the houses which have been engulfed by London and yet still, astonishingly, seems to be in a rural setting, an illusion largely created by the fact that Kew Gardens and the protected Park combine to form a green oasis.

There was a convent on the site here, founded by Henry v. James I gave it to Henry Percy, Duke of Northumberland, for whom Inigo Jones made some alterations. But it was Robert Adam who, between 1761 and 1770, transformed the uncompromising fifteenth-century building into a glowing jewel box of colours and carvings and marbles. Drawing upon the deep Northumberland purse, Adam was able to indulge his passion for Roman classicism, even to the extent of importing genuine Roman antiques. The ante-chamber is like a Roman temple, complete with statues. The Long Gallery was originally Jacobean until transformed by Adam: the Hall is another Roman setting in black and white marble with the additional luxury of ivory and gold and crimson silk.

PENSHURST PLACE, KENT

This is an excellent example of the great house as a kind of organic growth developing over the centuries, assimilating different styles and reflecting different customs. The Great Hall was built, about 1340, by John de Poultney, four times Lord Mayor of London and the chief financier of Edward's Crecy campaigns. It must have seemed daringly modern at the time, for it used the graceful, towering tracery of the newly evolved lancet window – but the hearth was still in the centre, where it remains to this day.

Sir John Devereux was licensed to fortify the house in 1393, and half a century later the second hall was added. Henry Sidney, brother-in-law of the doomed Earl of Leicester, took up residence here in 1567, doubtless reflecting in his turn on the ingratitude of monarchs. He occupied his time in giving a Tudor imprint to the house. But though the house still bears the shape he gave it, posterity remembers his name for a less tangible reason: it was at Penshurst that his son Philip was born – the son who, as poet, statesman and soldier, was to be the very mirror of the Christian knight before his death in battle at the age of 32.

KNOLE HOUSE, KENT

Few great houses have had their story told with such loving skill as Knole has had in that evocative book *Knole and the Sackvilles* by V. Sackville-West. The author was the daughter of the third Baron Sackville, disbarred from inheriting by the laws of succession and finding perhaps some compensation in turning the story of her home into one of the minor masterpieces of English literature.

Knole was the product of the first great wave of Jacobean opulence. Originally a palace of the Archbishops of Canterbury built in 1456, it was transformed internally by Thomas Sackville, first Earl of Dorset about 1603. Today, it is one of the largest private houses in England, externally resembling a walled city, astonishing in its sheer size. The visitor carries away an impression not so much of architectural beauty but of wealth – a riot of decoration and ornament-carvings, gildings, brocades, marbles tapestries. Every room has some unique treasure whether it is the Venetian Ambassador's room with its tapestries or the King's Room with the remarkable silver furniture of Charles II.

HEVER CASTLE, KENT

It was in 1526 that Henry VIII met the 19-year-old Anne Boleyn in Hever Castle and altered the course of English history as a result. The Castle must have looked the same then as it had done nearly two centuries earlier when it was built, and as it does today, four centuries afterward. It was built in the late thirteenth century by one of Edward I's knights, William de Hever, as a fortified manor house in the Eden valley. Anne's father, Sir Geoffrey Boleyn, bought it in 1457: he was probably intent on social climbing, for the Boleyn's belonged to that increasingly common class, the wealthy parvenu, and an aristocrat's castle gave a much-needed air of distinction to the family.

The castle was acquired in 1903 by the first Viscount Astor, who solved a standard problem in an unusual manner. Hever was not large enough to provide accommodation for the huge staff of the new owner. Instead of tinkering with the castle itself, however, Astor created what was virtually a separate village of Tudor-style houses and cottages, linked to the castle by a bridge across the moat.

WILTON HOUSE, WILTSHIRE

Wilton House is on the site of an Abbey which Henry VIII gave to the first Earl of Pembroke in 1541. The so-called Holbein Porch – now a garden house – is the only trace of the Tudor building which was one of the cultural centres of the country – the first performance of *As You Like It* took place there.

In 1633 the fourth Earl began what was to be the largest house to be erected during the uncertain Jacobean period: he was doubtless encouraged by the fat sinecures that the king bestowed on him. Isaac de Caus was the architect, but posterity rather unfairly gives all the credit to his famous assistant, Inigo Jones. The great fire of 1647, which destroyed most of the state rooms, gave Jones the opportunity to decorate throughout in his own rich style. He designed the so-called Double-Cube Room, reputed to be the noblest room in the kingdom and owing its name to the fact that its length is exactly twice its height and breadth. The room was built as a setting for ten of Van Dyke's great canvases, part of the treasures which the art-loving Pembrokes amassed during their long residence at Wilton.

LONGLEAT, WILTSHIRE

Beautiful in its own right, Longleat is also of great architectural importance, for it was the first great house to be built in the style of the English Renaissance. Its owner, Sir John Thynne, was a friend of Somerset, William Cecil, Sir Thomas Gresham, William Sharington of Lacock – a little band of bold cultural innovators all of whom were passionate amateur architects. Longleat took a generation to build for, begun in 1541, it was not completed until 1580. Thynne employed a number of architects and designers, but his was the single coordinating mind which put a unified impression on their work. The most obvious break with the past is created by the immense windows looking outward, instead of into an inner court, and the flat roof in place of the traditional ridges and gables. The interior was redecorated in the currently fashionable Italian style in the 1860s but the traditional Great Hall remains much as Thynne left it.

COTHELSTONE MANOR, SOMERSET

Here, the owner's prosperity has preserved a gem, unchanged, for posterity. In the closing years of the eighteenth century the last Lord Stawell turned his back on the modest manor house which had sheltered his family for over 700 years and set up home in the handsome new Cothelstone Park. The manor house remained, down by the village and the church. It was Cothelstone Park which felt the full force of nineteenth-century restoration: Cothelstone Manor looks today much as it did in the sixteenth century.

The Stawells came to Cothelstone in the wake of the Conqueror – a remarkably but not uniquely long tenure. The family even survived that time of troubles, the Commonwealth. The head of the house was a king's man and saw the inside of a gaol for his pains while the family was scattered far and wide. Stawell's wife was permitted to return and was allowed a modest income from the once wealthy estate – a few hundreds a year with which she kept things ticking over until her husband was released. Charles II made her son a baron after the Restoration and the Stawells picked up the rhythm of their tranquil life below the Quantock Hills as though the brief unpleasantness had never been.

PETWORTH HOUSE, SUSSEX

Petworth will ever be associated with the singularly unpleasant Charles Seymour, Duke of Somerset. He seems to have been almost pathologically snobbish: on his journeys from London outriders cleared the common folk from his path; he never addressed a servant directly and insisted on being served on bended knee.

He acquired Petworth by marrying the Percy heiress, Elizabeth, in 1682: although only 15 she had already been widowed twice, being treated simply as a dynastic pawn. Somerset began the massive rebuilding of Petworth in 1686 and finished ten years later. The identity of his architect has always been a mystery – he may, perhaps, have been the Dutchman Talman. By the end of the rebuilding the only thing that remained of the ancient Percy home was the thirteenth-century chapel. The vast main front is over 300 feet long, its chief interior feature being the superb Carved Room of Grinling Gibbons. Fire gutted the southern part of the house in 1714 – John Selden, a local carver, lost his life trying to save his carvings – but the beautiful, cool Marble Hall survived.

ARUNDEL CASTLE, SUSSEX

One of the most venerable of English castles, Arundel is nevertheless a home, the seat of the Dukes of Norfolk as it has been for the past 500 years. Earl Roger de Montgomery built the keep, drawbridge and barbican soon after the Conquest, the round shell keep – a rare example of a once common form – providing the nucleus from which everything else developed. The castle passed to the Fitzalans in the fourteenth century and then to Sir John Howard, created first Duke of Norfolk in 1483. He was also made Earl Marshal of England, creating the poignant situation whereby a Catholic stage-manages the coronation of a Protestant monarch.

Arundel Castle was largely destroyed in 1649 and the domestic quarters have been rebuilt several times since. The fifteenth Duke – whose passion for Gothic architecture created the great Catholic churches in Norwich and Arundel – reconstructed the castle in a thirteenth-century style.

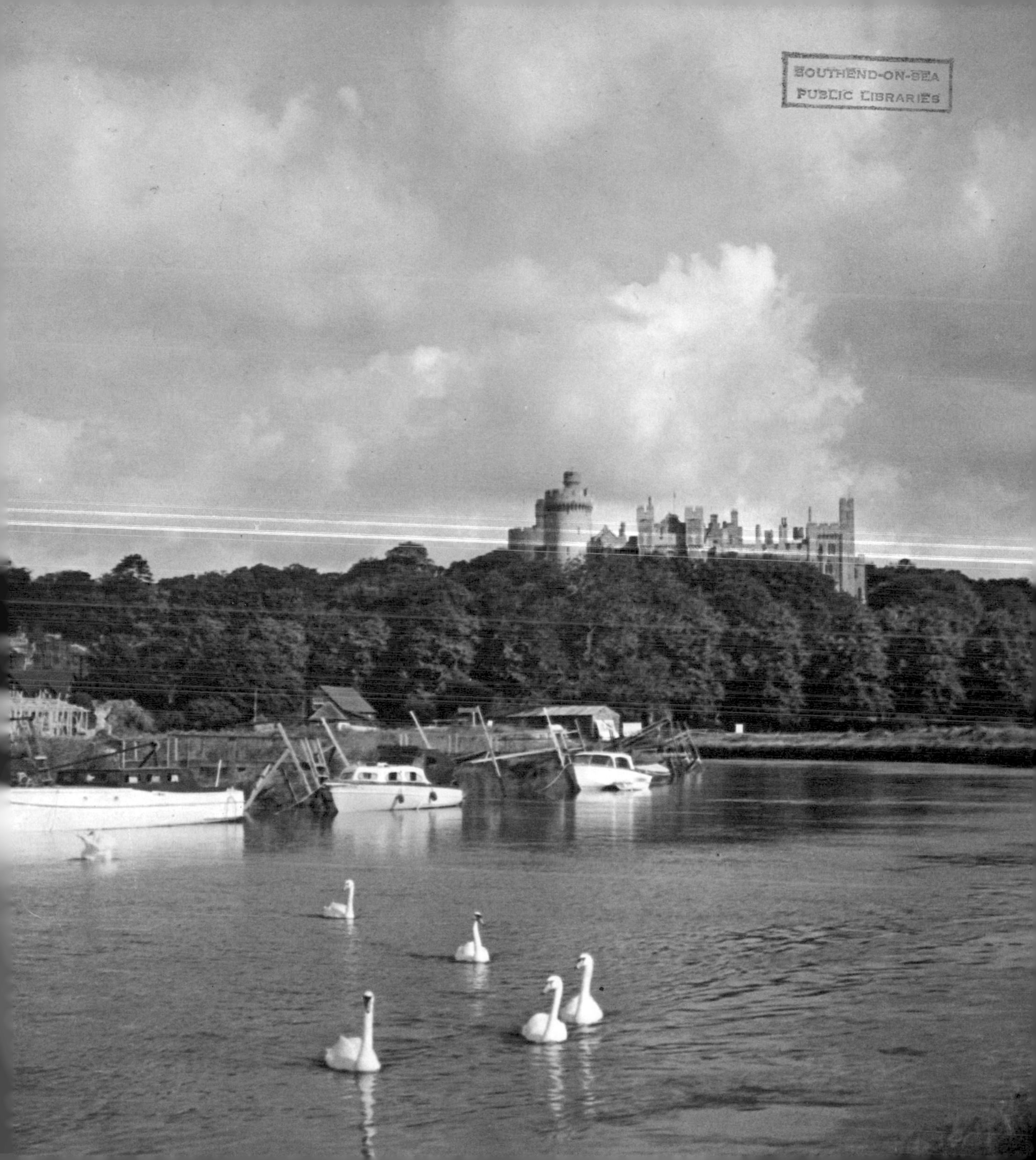